Preface

We burn through our bodies like candles in the heat of life, and for a short-lived time, we shine brilliantly. We burn like a Phoenix resurrected from ashes, like a thousand gasoline oceans set ablaze beneath a plutonium moon. We radiate the night like jubilant stars, embellishing the cosmos and devouring darkness whole.

That is, until the coldness of death overcomes us, and that fire which once burned so fervently, is slowly reduced to a flicker, a shimmer, and then to ashes. We fade away slow and melancholy, like lackluster stars of the morning – losing light in the glorious sun, passing from the earth and its adversity, only to be remembered by what we have done.

This is the reality of death; it is a cup that we all must drink from, a final taste of life's recurring bitter-sweetness. There is not a single living creature on earth, except that it will one day cease to exist, and soon embrace an eternal quietness.

Yet, there is an element of our being that is timeless, that is divine and undying. Irrespective of what happens to us in our lives, we carry within us this miracle, a seed of immortality, an eternal flame that transcends the flesh and supersedes the scheme of time.

The soul perceives the world beyond the veil of life and death; it sees the eternal luminous interconnectedness of all beings and things that undergird our manifest dimension. It recognizes the vast, empty openness of the transcendental ground shared by all beings.

The soul is the compass to the universe's deepest truth – the most confounding creature known to man. Its innuendos are gateways to further inquisitions. Its descriptions are elusive and absent of surety.

The soul is a maze of indefiniteness, a source of immense defeat and vexation to anyone who endeavours to capture its essence without the proper guidance, knowledge, and wisdom.

So, what is the soul? How can one render this mystifying phenomenon into the language of the common man? Where is it captured? And how are we to set it free? The answer is simple. *NO* ONE truly knows the function, purpose, or definite whereabouts of the soul. It is a matter only known to *Rabb*.

Yet, when you place a glass prism upon a windowsill and let the sun stream through it, a continuum of colours glisten on the floor. What we call "white" is in reality a rainbow of coloured rays packed into a tiny space; the prism sets them free. Imagine love as the white light of the soul; the prism that sets it free.

The purpose of this book is to make the essence of love perceptible to the human being, through the medium of Quran, the authentic Sunnah and art. May your soul be enlightened!

Mawadah

The Art of Interlocking Souls

Volume 1

Youssef Kromah
Mawadah: The Art of Interlocking of Souls
Volume 1

Cover Art by Tina Sta Cruz

ISBN: 978-1492827382
ISBN-13: 149282738X

Acknowledgements

All Praise is Due to Allah, Lord of the Worlds, Creator of the heavens, Earth and everything in between. I bear witness that there is no deity worthy of worship except Him, and that Muhammad (SAW) is His last and final Messenger. I am well aware that without God's divine love and mercy, none of my dreams could have ever come true. May His praise never abandon my lips.

I want to thank my mother, father and the entire Kromah family who believed, supported and encouraged my dreams, in spite of all the times it took me away from them. It has been a long and tasking journey for us all. May our family tree stand firm in the soil of *taqwa*, bending at times, but never to be broken.

Following, I would like to express my sincerest appreciation to Tina Sta Cruz, my graphic designer, for the breathtaking book cover she created, and for her invaluable time and patience. To the many people who saw me through this endeavor. To all of my friends, mentors, colleagues, educators and admirers that provided support, discussed critical ideas with me, read, wrote, offered comments, allowed me to quote their remarks and assisted me in the editing, proofreading and design of this manuscript. May this manuscript act as a *sadaqa jariyyah for us all*, and forever be the satisfying fruits of our labor.

Lastly, but not of all least, I offer my sincerest gratitude and indebtedness to my wife, Cyara Kromah, for spending her most valued time, effort and resources in the meticulous framing, development, and conclusion of this project. I love you beyond the jurisdiction of words. May our souls forever be intertwined.

Ameen

"All I wanted
All I ever wanted
Since the bones
In me began to grow
Was to know love
And for love
To know me."

Christopher Poindexter

Contents

Youssef Kromah

The Introduction

Prophet Muhammad (SAW) said in an authentic narration reported by Abu Hurayrah (RAA) that "Souls are like conscripted soldiers; those that recognize one another unite in harmony, and those that do not recognize one another are at aversion."

Ibn Hajar (RAA) mentioned in his commentary on the narration that perhaps what is being referred to here is the beginning of creation, in the realm of the unseen, when souls, as it was reported, existed before bodies, and frequently gathered together in the heavens to express their sentiments about the affairs of the future.

Later, when these same souls come into the physical realm of existence, and enter their human forms, they may recognize one another from an earlier realm, and interact on either hostile or genial terms based upon the preceding.

Abu Hatim (RAA) explained in his commentary that the grounds upon which people find concordance and harmony between themselves in this life – after the Decree – lies within the familiarity of the two souls. Contrastingly, the grounds whereupon other beings find enmity and hate between themselves, lies within the unfamiliarity of the two souls.

Hence, if two souls recognize one other from before, they will find warmth and affection between themselves, and if there was a sense of incongruity between the two souls from before, they will correspondingly find an oddity and peculiarity between their beings in this life.

Ibn `Abbas (RAA) once saw a man and said,

`Indeed he loves me.'

When asked, 'And how do you know?'

He said, 'Because I love him and souls are like conscripted soldiers, those that recognize one another unite in harmony, and those that do not recognize one another are at aversion.'

Qatadah mentioned the verses of Quran:

Had your Lord so willed, He could have surely made mankind one community, but as things subsist now, they will not cease to differ among themselves and follow erroneous ways, except for those who your Rabb places His mercy upon. And it is for this reason (freedom of choice) that He has created them.

[Quran, Hud: 118-119]

As for souls of light, their hearts and desires are unified, irrespective of how far they may be from each other in time and distance. As for souls of darkness, their hearts and desires are conflicted, irrespective of how close they may be to each other in time and distance. The paths of light and darkness have already been laid, and trotted many times over. In the end, the outcome is always the same. Light will always prevail.

Mansur al-Karizi said in a poem:

Whatever the eyes
and heart behold
will be in endearment.

For neither the heart nor the eyes
can be concealed,
but they are only two souls,
one in view of the other.

So one recognizes the other
and hence, they meet
in love and unison.

The greatest indication of what an individual is like in their daily affairs is demonstrated through who they befriend and who they are at enmity with.

I have never witnessed anything more indicative of another, even more so than smoke indicating fire, as much as I've seen a friend allude to the identity of their counterpart. Surely, each creature seeks it likeness, in similar waters similar fish are found, and birds of a feather forever flock together.

The sensitive soul avoids accompanying the insensitive one. It shies away from the soul whose nature is iniquitous. The soul does so with an astute awareness and cognizance of just how contagious and transmittable the character can be when left unheeded. Undoubtedly, you will find that whenever an individual remains in the company of another for an extended period of time, they will consciously or subconsciously begin to assume their characteristics.

Certainly, there are people in this world who if you were ever to meet, you would find an immediate attraction and allure to their character, and as the acquaintance grew further, so would the fondness and magnetism. Contrastingly, there are people in this world who if you were to ever meet, you would find an immediate repulse and aversion to their character, and as the acquaintance grew further, so would the discord and dissonance.

Knowledge of how to effectively govern and navigate these relationships will arise in the study of Mawadah: The Art of Interlocking Souls.

Chapter 1
To Love Rabb

"We need to find God, and He cannot be found in noise and restlessness. God is the friend of silence. See how nature – trees, flowers, grass grows in silence; see the stars, the moon and the sun, how they move in silence. We need silence to be able to touch souls."

~ Mother Theresa

The Meaning of 'Rabb'

Rabb is an Arabic word meaning Lord, Sustainer, Cherisher or Master, which in an Islamic context refers to Allah. The literal meaning of the word Rabb is Sustainer and Master. In that sense a man is the "rabb" of his house. From the same root stems the verb *yurabbi*, meaning "raise" – as in to raise a child. Yet, the actual meaning of Rabb is so vast, other languages lack an equivalent of the word.

Some have explained it to mean a fostering of things, in such a manner as to help them attain one condition after another, until they reach their goal of completion. Thus, it conveys not only the idea of raising up or nourishing, but also that of regulating, sustaining and bringing to maturity by way of development from the earliest state to that of the highest perfection. The Quran, in Surah Fatihah, introduces this name in the beginning, "All Praise is due to Allah, *Rabb* of all the worlds," thus stating clearly that Rabb nourishes and fosters everything that exists.

Why does the Love of Rabb come first in the Art of Interlocking Souls? Because when we place Rabb first in our lives, all things fall into the proper perspective. The love of Rabb will govern the claims of our affection, the demands on our time, the interests we pursue, and the order of our priorities.

We should place Rabb ahead of everyone and everything else in our lives. In order to truly love Rabb we must first reform our hearts and minds. When many people think of love, they think of the human emotional state, a selfish phenomenon in its essence—it loves when the conditions are right, or when it feels like loving. However, Rabb is not interested in any self-centered, self-seeking or self-absorbed form of love.

We do not love Rabb according to our feelings. Feelings are unstable, unsound and at any given moment subject to change. Rather, we love with our actions. When we obey Rabb's commandments, trust His Power, and accept His creed, only then, do we exhibit love.

The greatest right of Rabb, incumbent upon us all, is that we worship Him without associating any partners, and that we possess within us a firm belief in His Angels, Books, Messengers, The Day of Recompense and His Divine Decree. It is essential that we uphold an undying pursuit of human excellence, which encompasses the absolute perseverance and wherewithal to acquire a true knowledge of Rabb, to act upon this knowledge, and to enlighten others with patience. When we do this with sincerity, Rabb has made it binding upon Himself to give us sufficiency and success in the affairs of this world and the next.

The Art of Interlocking Souls testifies that the greatest of all actions is the pure love of Rabb—it never fails or falters, it endures forever, and without it we are left as aimless creatures wandering the world in a continuum of emptiness and futility. This is why it is paramount that we seek and be consumed by this love, so when this love appears, we shall be like it, and it like us.

Surah Hashr

﴿ يَأَيُّهَا الَّذِينَ ءَامَنُواْ اتَّقُواْ اللَّهَ وَلْتَنظُرْ نَفْسٌ مَّا قَدَّمَتْ لِغَدٍ وَاتَّقُواْ اللَّهَ إِنَّ اللَّهَ خَبِيرٌ بِمَا تَعْمَلُونَ وَلاَ تَكُونُواْ كَالَّذِينَ نَسُواْ اللَّهَ فَأَنسَهُمْ أَنفُسَهُمْ أُوْلَئِكَ هُمُ الْفَسِقُونَ ﴾

18. O you who believe! Have consciousness of Allah, and let every person look to what he has put forth for tomorrow. And be conscious of Allah, verily He is All-Aware of what you do.

19. And be not like those who forgot Allah, and He caused them to forget themselves. Those are truly the rebellious ones.

Invocation of Love

O Rabb, place upon my heart love, and upon my tongue love, and within my ears love, and in my sight love, and above me love, and below me love, and to my right love, and to my left love, and to my front love, and to my rear love. O Rabb, place love in my soul and love in its mate. Place love in my fate. Place love in my face. Place love in my family and love in my race. O Rabb, provide me for love, magnify for me love, magnetize for me love. Let love make me and me make love. O Rabb, grant me divine love, sublime love, unconfined love, untimed love, an undying love. O Rabb, place love in my blood, and love in my veins, place love in my calling and love in my name. O Rabb, make love of my days and love of my nights. Make love of my life, and love of my flesh, and love of my bones, and love of my death. O Rabb, increase me in love, and increase me in love, and increase me in love. O Rabb, grant me love, upon love, upon love, upon love.

Of Men & Memory

Who are you?

Where are you?

When are you?

Why are you?

Remember Rabb

So much so

That you- yourself

Are forgotten

Who are you?

Where are you?

When are you?

Why are you?

Remember Rabb

So much so

That you – yourself

Are remembered

Who are you?

Where are you?

When are you?

Why are you?

Remember Rabb

And The Soul's
Mate Echoed

A woman's heart should be so lost in God
That a man would have to seek Him
To find her

A man's heart should be so lost in God
That a woman would have to seek Him
To find him

Before I began searching for her heart
I knew her heart was searching for God

Before I began searching for his heart
I knew his heart was searching for God

Before I ever found her love
I knew her love had found God

Before I ever found his love
I knew his love had found God

Before I ever believed in her heart
I knew her heart believed in God

Before I ever believed in his heart
I knew his heart believed in God

Before I loved her for the sake of myself
I loved her for the sake of God

Before I loved him for the sake of myself
I loved him for the sake of God

It was through seeking God
That I found her

It was through seeking God
That I found him

It was through seeking her
That I found God

It was through seeking him
That I found God

Love Letter To Rabb

Dear Rabb,

If I spent an entire lifetime pondering Your Attributes, it wouldn't be enough to satisfy my yearning. Drawing closer to You dispels the darkness of ignorance prevailing within my soul. True knowledge of You is the key to security and tranquility within my inner being. I love You because I know if I draw near to You a hand's span, You draw near to me an arm's length, and if I draw near to You an arm's length, You draw near to me a fathom's length. By contrast, I must consider my steps carefully before drawing close to any human being. If I love a human being overly, he or she may humiliate me, and even grow more averse to me, rather than reciprocate my love and compassion. I love You Rabb, because You are the Eternal and Everlasting. No matter how deeply my heart becomes attached to You, there is no fear that one day I will be distressed by Your death or absence. You are free of such imperfection.   I love You Rabb, for showing me such affection while You are self-sufficient, and rich beyond need, while it is I who stands in need of You. Your door is constantly ajar and welcoming, whereas the doors of kings are closed. As for You, the Almighty Creator, the King of Kings, we can meet You whenever we like, day and night, through prayer and supplication. You never grow annoyed with our frequent invocations. You grant our requests and even reward us for asking. What a Merciful, Glorious and Loving God. May Your praise never abandon my lips. I love You Rabb.

Love,
Your Servant

Chapter 2
To Love Umm

"A mother is the truest friend we have, when trials heavy and sudden fall upon us; when adversity takes the place of prosperity; when friends desert us; when trouble thickens around us, still will she cling to us, and endeavor by her kind precepts and counsels to dissipate the clouds of darkness, and cause peace to return to our hearts."

~Washington Irving

A man came
to the Prophet Muhammad (SAW)
one day and asked Him,

'O Messenger of God!
Who among the people is most
worthy of my good companionship?

The Prophet (SAW) said: Your mother.

The man said, 'Then who?'

The Prophet (SAW) said: Then your mother.

The man further asked, 'Then who?'

The Prophet (SAW) said again: Then your
mother.

The man asked again, 'Then who?'

The Prophet (SAW) said: Then your father.

[Bukhari, Muslim]

The Meaning of 'Umm'

The Arabic word Umm that is used for mother means the root and the foundation of a thing. However, it is so widely used to mean mother, that its other meanings are very seldom ever acknowledged.

To be an Umm is one of Rabb's greatest gifts. There is no man walking on earth, from the most honored of men to the most debased of his kind, except that he once lay as a helpless, innocent baby in a woman's arms and was dependent on her love and care for his existence. It is Umm who rocks the cradle of the world and holds the first affections of mankind. She possesses a power beyond that of a king on his throne. Umm stands for all that is pure, kind and noble. She who does not make the world better for having lived in it has failed to be all that an Umm should be.

There is nothing more absolute or enduring than Umm's love. Umm's love is proudly unconditional; it is warm, comforting, sympathetic and exceedingly pervasive.

Its colossal and larger than life nature cannot be contained, constrained or controlled. Its presence grants the one loved a sense of comfort; its absence produces a sentiment of bewilderment and utter despair.

The right of your mother is that you acknowledge that she carried you where no one carries anyone, and she fed you with the fruit of her heart – that which no one feeds anyone, and she protected you with her hearing, sight, arms, hands, legs, skin and all of her internal organs. She was highly delighted to do so, to sacrifice all of her being for your sake, without even a second thought. She did not care if she went hungry as long as you ate. If she was naked, as long as you were clothed. If she was thirsty, as long as you drank. If she was in the sweltering heat, as long as you were in the shade. If she was weary, as long as you were resting. Her abdomen was your abode, her breast was your sustenance, and her womb was your fort. Praise Rabb for the miracle of Umm's love and mercy.

Surah Ahqaf

﴿وَوَصَّيْنَا الإِنسَنَ بِوَلِدَيْهِ إِحْسَاناً حَمَلَتْهُ أُمُّهُ كُرْهاً وَوَضَعَتْهُ كُرْهاً وَحَمْلُهُ وَفِصَلُهُ ثَلاَثُونَ شَهْراً حَتَّى إِذَا بَلَغَ أَشُدَّهُ وَبَلَغَ أَرْبَعِينَ سَنَةً قَالَ رَبِّ أَوْزِعْنِي أَنْ أَشكُرَ نِعْمَتَكَ الَّتِي أَنْعَمْتَ عَلَيَّ وَعَلَى وَلِدَيَّ وَأَنْ أَعْمَلَ صَلِحاً تَرْضَهُ وَأَصْلِحْ لِي فِي ذُرِّيَّتِي ﴾

15. And We have enjoined on man to be dutiful and kind to his parents. His *Umm* bears him with hardship. And she delivers him with hardship. And the weaning of him is thirty months, till when he attains full strength and reaches forty years, he says:

"My Lord! Grant me the power and ability that I may be grateful for Your favor which You have bestowed upon me and upon my parents, and that I may do righteous good deeds, such as to please You, and make my offspring good.

Youssef Kromah

The Morning of
My Morning

I woke up this morning and

Fell mind over body in love

With my mother's face

For the very first time

Since yesterday

Fell mind over body in love

With the way her skin

Smells of sunbeams

For the very first time

Since yesterday

I remembered

Where God placed heaven

With the way her skin

Smells of sunbeams

I wonder how long it took to digest the Sun

I remembered where God placed heaven

Seven skies beneath her feet

I wonder how long it took her to digest the Sun

If it took her nine months to set me free

Her son

Seven skies beneath her feet

Ummi

I can smell you in my dreams

Last night, I fell asleep

With a handful of prayer

And I woke up this morning

With my mother's face

Thank God

Nickname

When I was a child,
Ummi nicknamed me Poppy.
She knew I'd be dope.

Saving Grace

Super Woman.

You arrived just in time to save me.

You caught me – falling out of orbit

like a paralyzed planet, all tremble and

murmur, with Katrina levies for limbs. Two

seconds shy of disaster, you caught me and

held me like a prayer in the tender of your

palms. Umm, your love feels like healing –

hooked umbilical cord to naval – the way you

nurtured me to life. In a body of darkness, the

way you nurtured me to light. It could've been

the heaven in your hello, the halo set in your

smile or the haven in your arms. You must be

an ayah from Quran. Inna ma'aal usree yusraa.

The ease that follows hardship. The quiet

before the storm. A Bedouin's last sip of water.

Both kryptonite and crystal. Super woman and

savior. I don't know whether to hate you for

taking so long, or love you for being just on

time. Yes, you were just on time, and you

saved me. My Super Woman – my Ummi.

Love Letter To Umm

Dear Umm,

You know, my dear Umm, as the entire universe knows, that you are the embodiment of God's love and mercy here on Earth. You alone hold the heavens beneath the heels of your feet. I am forever indebted to you for the way you've raised me into a man of such tenderness, compassion and benevolence. For it was in the softness of your womb that I first learned the language of love; that voice which expresses the inner sentiments of the heart, and whispers its passionate secrets to the worthy listener. It spoke to me with all the sweetness and delicacy of speech, with a boldness of expression beyond anything in this universe. Know Umm, that I possess a love for you so deep, it would drown an ocean, if you willed it. I shall seal this letter with a prayer for you, forever praising Rabb in your stunning name. I love you Umm.

Love,
Your Son

Chapter 3
To Love Abb

"A man's worth is measured by how he parents his children, by what he gives them, what he keeps away from them, the lessons he teaches them, and the lessons he allows them to learn on their own. My father gave me the greatest gift anyone could ever give another person: he believed in me, and taught me to believe in myself."

~Lisa Rogers

The Meaning of 'Abb'

Abb is the Arabic term for father. Abb or Abu may also be used as a *kunya*, an honorary title. To refer to a man or woman by their kunya is courteous in Arab and Islamic culture, so that Abu takes on the function of praise. I.e. Abu Youssef, *the Father of Youssef.*

There is nothing more sobering or judicious than Abb's love. It is silent, strengthening, and dependably steadfast. Due to its unyielding nature, it cannot be conformed, compromised or conned. Abb's love is an earned and deserved love; it is a love based upon expectation and duty. Abb's love tends to punish and reward, to set limits, to guide, and to demand obedience. Abb's love is a love that judges and holds to account, therefore it provokes, it enlightens, it cultivates, it disciplines, and it inspires. Part of the child's nature is the understanding of obedience and submission. Many of us learn discipline, self-control, and restraint through the early rearing of Abb.

The right of your Abb is that you should know that he is your root, and you are his branch – and without him and the mercy of Rabb, you would not be. Whenever you see something in yourself which pleases you, you should know that your Abb is the root of its blessing upon you. The existence of the child is dependent on the existence of their Abb. The success of the child is contingent on the presence and activeness of the Abb. This should act as a reminder to fathers and children alike, as to the immense importance of the Abb in the life of the child.

An ideal Abb, and by ideal I mean an Abb who is present and active, has the ability to change almost every social problem we now find ourselves facing. I'd be assumptive enough to even say that there isn't a single type of crime or crisis so big that it couldn't be fixed or wiped out if every Abb would just step up. Certainly, both parents are essential – but an emphasis on fathering is necessary because of the enormity of its absence.

Surah Hajj

﴿ وَجَاهِدُوا فِي اللَّهِ حَقَّ جِهَادِهِ هُوَ اجْتَبَكُمْ وَمَا جَعَلَ عَلَيْكُمْ فِي الدِّينِ مِنْ حَرَجٍ مِّلَّةَ أَبِيكُمْ إِبْرَهِيمَ هُوَ سَمَّكُمُ الْمُسْلِمِينَ مِن قَبْلُ وَفِي هَذَا لِيَكُونَ الرَّسُولُ شَهِيداً عَلَيْكُمْ وَتَكُونُواْ شُهَدَآءَ عَلَى النَّاسِ فَأَقِيمُواْ الصَّلَوةَ وَءَاتُواْ الزَّكَوةَ وَاعْتَصِمُواْ بِاللَّهِ هُوَ مَوْلَكُمْ فَنِعْمَ الْمَوْلَى وَنِعْمَ النَّصِيرُ ﴾

78. And strive hard in Allah's way as you ought to strive. He has chosen you, and has not laid upon you in religion any hardship. It is the religion of your *father* Abraham.

He has named you Muslims, both before and in this (Qur'an) that the Messenger may be a witness over you and you be witnesses over mankind! So, perform the prayer, give the tides and hold fast to Allah. He is your Friend, what an Excellent Friend and what an Excellent Helper is He!

Youssef Kromah

The Sky of My Son

There is a man
Who I love – beyond
The jurisdiction of words

There is a man
Who loves me – back
Beyond the province of time

Before this sun
Even sought to rise,
This man was his sky;
Was the cumulus clouds
That embellished his shine

This man was the earth,
Was the trees, was the wood,
Was the work, was the axes

This man was the mountain
That slowed the world
From spinning off its axis
This man was Atlas
To the burdens of his son

This man was an atlas
To the inquiries of his son

This man is
The one who I love – beyond
The jurisdiction of words
The one who loves me back – beyond
The province of time

Before this sun
Even sought to rise,
This man was his sky;
Was the cumulus clouds
That embellished his shine

This man was the earth,
Was the trees, was the wood,
Was the work, was the axes

This man was the mountain
That slowed the world
From spinning off its axis

This man was Atlas to the burdens of his son
This man was an atlas to the inquires of his son
This man was, is, and forever will be My *Abb*

Of Fathers and Souls

(Some) Fathers are like souls:

Even though you can't see them,

Somewhere, they exist.

Saving Face

As I peer into the eyes of the man who I know to be my father, I see nothing but myself. I see a spitting image of me standing before my very own eyes, as if I am him in present tense, and he is the me of the future; the me I have yet to become. I am stunned by this man's eyes, his brows, his nose and his smile – the way they so resemble mine. My God, this man's face looks just like mine. His movement, his temperament, his upright disposition – indistinguishable from mine. The way he kneels before God and towers before men. The way he thinks in stark truth and sets his will in pen. I sense my own essence in this man, and I am proud of the me I am in the future. The man I am soon to become. Come tomorrow, this man and I will be one.

Love Letter To Abb

Dear Abb,

I will forget myself before I ever forget the man that taught, guided, and instilled wisdom in me my entire life. You have sworn to me countless times that you love me by your actions. You have sworn to me countless times that you will never leave me by your presence. You have sworn to me a blessed and righteous life by your teaching me Islam. You are the gravity that keeps my world in place. I pray one day to be half the father you have been to me. I pray that when my children need something, I am there for them as you have been for me. I pray that when they have questions, I am there for them as you have been for me. I pray that when they are going through pleasant or trying times, that I am there for them, just as you have always been there for me. I pray Rabb blesses and increases you for raising me to be upright. I love you dearly Abb.

Love,
Your Son

Chapter 4
To Love Ummah

"Love is our most unifying and empowering common spiritual denominator. The more we ignore its potential to bring greater balance and deeper meaning to human existence, the more likely we are to continue to define history as one long inglorious record of man's inhumanity to man."

~Alberjhani

One of the unique features about the religion of Islam is that it is a religion of unity – even more, it is a uniting faith, to the full extent of the word. It stands for the unity of gods into one supreme God – Allah; for the unity of the message brought by the messengers and Prophets: LA *ILAHA ILA* ALLAH – *There is no God worthy of worship but Allah*, for the unity of the spiritual and material sides of the individual into an integrated whole – the human being; for the unity of the earth and heavens into one universe; for the unity of the present world and the world to come; for the unity of all human beings in their origin – a single male–Adam, and his wife–Eve; and for the unity of all believers into one believing Ummah. This last aspect of unity – unity of the believers and the implications of "one Ummah" is the most essential notion to mankind.

An examination of the Qur'an reveals that the word Ummah is mentioned 49 times; the two words "one Ummah" are repeated a total of nine times.

The Meaning of 'Ummah'

The Arabic word *Ummah* is sometimes translated as *nation,* or *community.* It comprises those individuals who have something basic in common among them. All the messengers and Prophets of God belonged to one and the same Ummah because they had the same creed, religion, and message.

Islam binds the hearts of all believers and joins us in one Ummah. It protects us against weakness and disunity, and against failure and loss. The objective of the united Ummah of the believers is to worship one God, in the broad sense of worship, to deeper form da'awah (a unified call) to God, and to work for the realization of the religion of God.

The bond that binds the members of this Ummah is iman (faith). It is, and should be, stronger than all other bonds such as race, color, or national origin. It is even stronger than blood relationships. The stronger the iman, the stronger is the bond between the members of the Ummah.

The true and sincere believer shares the worries, happiness, and sorrow, of other believers, as is described by the following prophetic saying:

مثل المؤمنين فى توادهم
وتراحمهم وتعاطفهم مثل الجسد
اذا اشتكى منه عضو تداعى له
سائر الجسد بالسهر والحمى .

The similitude of the believers in their kindness, love, and affection, in their mercifulness, and in their sympathy and compassion towards one another, is like a body, when one organ ails, the entire body suffers. This suffering is born from the profound love and compassion for ummah the believer harbors in the soul.

We are all equal in the fact that we are all different. We are united by the reality that all colors and all cultures are distinct and individual. We are harmonious in the reality that we are all held to this earth by the same gravity. We may not share blood, but we share the air that keeps us alive.

Surah Imran

﴿ وَاعْتَصِمُواْ بِحَبْلِ اللَّهِ جَمِيعاً وَلاَ تَفَرَّقُواْ
وَاذْكُرُواْ نِعْمَةَ اللَّهِ عَلَيْكُمْ إِذْ كُنتُمْ أَعْدَآءً فَأَلَّفَ
بَيْنَ قُلُوبِكُمْ فَأَصْبَحْتُم بِنِعْمَتِهِ إِخْوَاناً وَكُنتُمْ
عَلَى شَفَا حُفْرَةٍ مِّنَ النَّارِ فَأَنقَذَكُم مِّنْهَا كَذلِكَ
يُبَيِّنُ اللَّهُ لَكُمْ ءَايَتِهِ لَعَلَّكُمْ تَهْتَدُونَ ﴾

103. And hold firmly to the rope of Allah, all together, and do not become divided. And remember the favor of Allah upon you – when you were enemies and He brought your hearts together, and you became, by His favor, brothers. And you were on the edge of a pit of the Fire, and He saved you from it. Thus does Allah makes clear to you His verses that you may be guided.

Manifesto of Mankind

Let today be the day that we emancipate our minds from the tyranny of mental slavery and truly embrace our manifest destiny.

Let every man, woman and child bear witness that we are equal in birth, divided only by the corrupting structures of man and society.

Now is the time to lift the veil of ignorance from our eyes and to embrace the burning illuminations of truth and justice; to find ourselves in our neighbors, and recognize the shared value of human life.

Now is the time to uproot the plagues of poverty, inequality, violence, drug addiction, alcoholism and mass incarceration from the broken systems that be, and to stop their poison from seeping into the roots of our communities.

We will stand in togetherness, as a people empowered and enlightened in knowledge, united behind the common good of man, and as firm believers in the universality of human excellence.

We will refuse to participate in any phenomenon destructive to ourselves, to our communities, and to our futures.

We have chosen to dwell in a place where only writers matter, where righteous matters, where righters matter. Mind over matter, and matter under mind.

We have chosen to fight by the medium of words, poems, stories and art; the ink of the scholar over the blood of the martyr.

Speak with wisdom, act with purpose. Let us run to our destiny like we are running out of time. We are all of one nature – and for that nature we strive.

Humans find purpose that in purpose is derived. There is one human race and until we are ALL free, no ONE shall have peace of mind.

Let today be the day that we emancipate our minds from the tyranny of mental slavery and truly embrace our manifest destiny.

There is no YOU; there is no I; there is only US.

...with help from Conor Coleman

A Virtuous Woman

Who can find a virtuous woman? A woman consumed by the *Creator* of all things rather than the things *created*, a woman God conscious, God fearing and God loving. A virtuous woman, a woman woven from the fabric of Maryam, of Asiyah, of Khadijah, and Fatimah bint Muhammad. Who can find a virtuous woman? For her worth cannot be measured in silver, or gold, or platinum. She is rarity. She is rhodium. She is the Earth's black gold, petroleum. She is the backbone of the great men behind the podium. She is ever observing and preserving; she is sodium to all that God holds sacred. An odium of opium, her Highness is natural. She is the gravity that stills the world on its axle. She is self-aware, self-assured, and self-loving. She is the soul of wherever she resides.

Her grace is simple, but to describe it would be a lie. Who can find a virtuous woman? For her worth cannot be measured in silver, or gold, or platinum. She is rarity. She is rhodium. She is the peace in pandemonium. Her wisdom is a well, deep and dense as osmium. She is upright and honored and absent of opprobrium. A praise appropriate for the praiseworthy and the slave worthy of the Most High. She is the insignia of human excellence, an evidence for the incredulous that virtue does exist. Who can find a virtuous woman? Favor is deceitful, and beauty is vain, but a woman that fears the LORD, shall forever be praised. Who can find a virtuous woman?

Vanity

Vanity struck the pose, stood there blasé and opposed to her suitor's embellished jargon.

She begged no pardon. Her heart carved in a symbol of the skeptic, dubious and haughty. Naughty not by nature, but rather by incantation, and the implantation of Satan's dogmas. Believed her not in God or karma. Instead she prayed upon the gaze of the eyes that preyed upon her. She was that sort of beautiful, pulchritudinous even. Believed in naught, but the thought of her own physical perfection, an obsession with such utter correction, unparalleled symmetry, precision and absence of fallacy. Flawless biology. She considered herself the center of the galaxy. Gallivanting about in all of her gaud, glory, and grandeur. Chin tilted towards the sky, not like a God, but like a woman who considered herself so. Oblivious of the misfortune soon to unfold. Vanity struck the pose, kneeled there attentive and imposed to her suitor's embellished jargon. She begged his pardon.

Narcissist

Narcissist struck the pose, stood there blasé and opposed to his Creator's divine jargon. He begged no pardon. His heart carved in a symbol of the skeptic, anti-empathetic, dubious and haughty. Naughty not by nature, but rather by incantation, and the implantation of Satan's dogmas. Believed him not in God or conscience. Instead he prayed upon the gaze of the eyes that preyed upon him. He was that sort of pompous, blasphemous even. Believed in naught, but the thought of his own physical perfection, an obsession with such utter correction, exactitude and absence of fallacy. Considered himself the center of the galaxy. He stood there gleaming in all of his gaud, glory, and grandeur. Chin tilted towards the sky, not like a God, but like a man who considered himself so. Little did he know. Narcissism struck the pose, kneeled there humbled and imposed to his Creator's enlightened jargon. He begged for pardon.

Love Letter To Ummah

Dear Ummah,

I have not forgotten.

I have not forgotten about Syria,

I have not forgotten about Pakistan,

I have not forgotten about Bosnia,

I have not forgotten about Somalia,

I have not forgotten about China,

I have not forgotten about India,

I have not forgotten about Nigeria,

I have not forgotten about Palestine,

I have not forgotten about Tunisia,

I have not forgotten about Egypt,

I have not forgotten about Libya,

I have not forgotten about Sudan,

I have not forgotten about Iraq,

I have not forgotten about Iran,

I have not forgotten about Yemen,

I have not forgotten about Afghanistan,

I have not forgotten about Bahrain,

I have not forgotten about Chechnya,

I have not forgotten about you my Ummah,

I have not forgotten about you my family,

As I sit in the comfort
And security of my home,
You are suffering, you are bleeding,
You are dying and begging
Not to be forgotten.
We have not forgotten you.
May you find ease,
And tranquility,
In the remembrance
Of us remembering you.

Love,
Your Brother in Islam

Chapter 5
To Know Self

"We are unknown to ourselves, we men of knowledge – and understandably so. We have never sought ourselves – how could it happen that we should ever find ourselves? We travel all over the world to marvel at the heights of mountains, at the vast compass of the ocean, at the circular motions of the stars, and we pass by ourselves every day without a second thought."

Unknown

Many of us go through our entire lives hardly scratching the surface of our actual identities. That is, we fail to truly dig deep into our thoughts, emotions, actions and motives. Part of the complication is that we are always in motion; constantly on the go, seeking the next task to complete, or the next obstacle to conquer. When to-do lists keep swelling, self-exploration becomes second priority, and it slowly fades into the backdrop of our lives. How can it not, when we never find time for the examination and development of ourselves.

Knowing yourself is a slow, deep, and strenuous process. It is long, winding, and tiresome. We must be prepared to travel it at all times. It brings you face-to-face with your doubts, anxieties, and insecurities. You will need every modicum of patience, courage, and faith you can muster up. Nevertheless, the journey of seeking self is one that rewards in abundance; it is the magnificent experience of watching the rose blossoming before your very own eyes.

Knowing yourself means knowing your values in life; your morals, beliefs, doubts, likes, dislikes, pros, cons and biases. Knowing your role in your own life, as well as in the life of others. Knowing yourself means understanding your strengths and weaknesses, your passions and fears. It means being aware of your quirks and idiosyncrasies, your tolerances and limits. It means knowing your deepest insecurities and suspicions.

Knowing yourself also means knowing your purpose in life. You are not born knowing yourself, and you certainly do not get to know yourself just by growing up and growing old. Knowing yourself is a conscious effort; you do it with intention, purpose, and perseverance.

Not knowing yourself becomes obvious sooner or later. A quiet frustration lives in your heart when you are ignorant to who you are. You can choose to live with this sentiment and ignore it, or you can begin the life-long process of getting to know yourself.

Surah Nisaa

﴿ وَذَكِّرْ فَإِنَّ الذِّكْرَى تَنفَعُ الْمُؤْمِنِينَ – وَمَا

﴿يَأَيُّهَا النَّاسُ اتَّقُواْ رَبَّكُمُ الَّذِى خَلَقَكُم مِّن

نَّفْسٍ وَحِدَةٍ وَخَلَقَ مِنْهَا زَوْجَهَا وَبَثَّ مِنْهُمَا

رِجَالاً كَثِيراً وَنِسَآءً وَاتَّقُواْ اللَّهَ الَّذِى تَسَآءَلُونَ

بِهِ وَالاُْرْحَامَ إِنَّ اللَّهَ كَانَ عَلَيْكُمْ رَقِيباً ﴾

1. Oh mankind! Have consciousness of your Lord, Who created you from a single soul, and from it He created its mate, and from them both He created many men and women, and have consciousness of Allah through Whom you demand your mutual rights, and reverence the wombs (that bore you). Surely, Allah is always watching over you.

Of Men & Foil

I, myself
Am full of all things good
It is what I consume
That seeks to destroy me

I, myself
Am fooled by all things good
It is what I presume
That seeks to destroy me

I, myself
Am foil of all things good
It is what's in my womb
That seeks to destroy me

I, myself am full
I, myself am fooled
I, myself am foil

A Light Reminder

Each star is a mirror
reflecting the truth inside you.

The night's sky is the place
where you keep your secrets.

You are the center
of someone's galaxy.

Your midnight
is someone else's noon.
Your sun
Is someone else's moon.

At the height of your own excellence,
you speak diamonds and pearls
into existence.

True love of self
is the only thing necessary
for you to survive.

12 Things to Ask Yourself

1. What is the one thing that makes you special and unique?

There is no other person on this planet quite exactly like you. For just a moment, quit focusing on what you are not, what you wish to be, or what others expect from you and find out what is the one thing you already have that makes you special. Identify your "special"-ness, acknowledge it, respect it and make it central to how you carry yourself.

2. How do people perceive you?

Do people see you for the special person that you are? Do they appreciate your unique abilities? If not, what is the reason? How can you change it? We judge ourselves by what we feel capable of doing, while others judge us by what we have already done.

How can you bridge the gap between what you are uniquely capable of being and the person that you currently are?

3.   If money was not a constraint, what would you be doing with your time?

Write a book? Become a poet? Grow a beautiful garden? Spend more time with your family? Take your time. Feel free to daydream. Once you have the vision in your mind, think of what is the one thing you can do now to move just one step closer to that vision. When you have a vision and start taking action, the universe will conspire to make it a reality.

4.   What do you do for a living?

There is nothing deep about this question. It really is as simple as it sounds. If your answer matches (or will lead you towards) what you answered to the previous question, you are on the right track. If you answered "Become a writer" above and "I am an engineer" to this one, you need to figure out how bridge the two. Maybe you can start a tech blog or a series of books about the adventures of engineering. Whatever the case, you can figure it out from there.

5.   What are you grateful for?

How long did you have to think to answer that question? If you answer was not immediate – if the images of your family and friends, your health, your ability to see, hear, walk and talk did not come to your mind instantly, you should start looking into developing an attitude of gratitude. Recollect the quote – "I cried because I had no shoes until I met a man who had no feet."

6.   If you die tomorrow, will you be happy with the life you've lived?

I don't want to sound morbid, but it's true -- you really could die tomorrow. Have you lived a good life? Have you left good memories to last your kids a lifetime? Have you forgiven everyone who has wronged you and have you asked for forgiveness from everyone you have wronged?

7.   What is the one movie you don't mind watching over and over? (Or the one book you could just read any number of times?)

The human mind responds strongly to narratives, so the story that touches you the most is the one that can tell you a lot about yourself. Or the one that you aspire your life to be like. What is the story that you don't mind watching/reading over and over again? What is the underlying theme/premise of the story?

8.   If someone made a movie out of your life, what will it be like?

Everybody has a story -- what is yours? Would the story of your life be filled with melodrama, self-pity, hatred, anger or frustration; or would it be a story about inner peace, happiness, love, growth, joy and transcendence?

If you are happy with your answer, keep doing what you are doing. If not, a quote by Maria Robinson may be of help -- "Nobody can go back and start a new beginning, but anyone can start today and make a new ending."

Who are your friends and foes?

9.   If you were in a sinking ship with everyone you know, and you could only save 10 people, who would it be?

A lot of us don't even realize who the most important people in our lives are. We constantly try to impress random people who hardly care about us, at the expense of neglecting those that matter the most to us. Are you aware of the handful of people that really mean something to you? Are you treating them right?

10.   If you die today, who will miss you the most?

Now, flip that around -- who are the people that have you on their list of most cherished people? You don't have to have led a life that warrants a national holiday when you die (though, that would be awesome!), but are you leaving behind a legacy that at least a handful of people will cherish?

11.   What will they say in your eulogy?

Why will these people miss you when you are gone? Will they read your eulogy out of rote and move on with their lives, will they choke up unable to continue, or will they smile all the way through because you showed them life is to be celebrated?

Who will you become?

12.   Are you a better person today than you were yesterday? Or the day before?

The source of a lot of misery in our lives is because we keep comparing our worst moments with the best of those around us. The only way to break out of this is to change your reference for comparison. Are you a better person today than you were before? Are you on a path of growth? Are you moving forward, standing still, or slipping backwards?

Who are you?

Love Letter to Self

Dear Self,

Somehow, you have wedged yourself in between my bones; I'd like to keep you here. I love you. I love the parts of you that you have yet to love. I love your tired symphony, the one you rewrite constantly, the one kept lodged in your torso for safe keeping. I love your trivialities; the ones you have weaved into poems for fear of losing them. I love your edges, the ones that feel coarse to the untrained hand, and the ones you think no one could ever love. I love the wrecks, breaks, and aches of you. I know that our world keeps turning us in different directions, but if you pick a space to stand in, I'll make sure to tether us to the ground and keep us steady. Keep us whole, and keep us ready. I'll take the heavy parts. I'll drape them in honey, ready to cover your skin with my own, but not to smother you. I just want to spread a thin layer of myself over you. Enough to keep you warm. I love you truly.

Love,

Your Self

Chapter 6
To Know Self-Less

"Perhaps, this is what love has always been, whether it is for man, woman or a cause -- the readiness to give and not ask for anything in return, the unquestioning willingness to lose everything, even if that loss is as something as precious as life itself."

~ F. Sinoli Jose

Many of us spend our entire lives thinking of only ourselves; our needs, wants, and desires. Very seldom do we take out the time to think of other people's feelings, needs, or even how our actions may affect them. If we wish to be selfless, the first thing that we must do is change our mindset.

At first, you will need to make a point of putting others first and thinking less of yourself. As time goes on, you will begin to reflexively think of others and it will become like second nature to you. This change is a process and will not happen overnight. People who are naturally selfless don't need anyone to remind them to help others, they instinctively know and this is the intended outcome.

A great way to learn selflessness is to begin doing good deeds whenever the opportunity arises. Doing small deeds for others like holding the door open for people behind you, helping an elder across the street or donating to a charity is very effective and will train you to be altruistic.

The idea is to do these good deeds for both people you know and perfect strangers; simply out of the kindness of your heart, without expecting anything back in return. By doing these small deeds you will be able to practice how to help others and how to notice when a person is in need of help. You will also be able to see how good it feels to help others and this will likely encourage you to do more.

Give to others. Selfless people are not stingy with their money or material goods and they are able to separate the material things in life from the more important things. A selfless person may give a stranger the coat off of his back because he realizes the burden of others, so he sees the need and gives.

We cannot live for ourselves alone. Our lives are connected by a thousand invisible threads and along these sympathetic fibers, our actions run as causes and return to us as results. Some call it karma, I call it Qadr. In the end, your actions will always come back to visit you – make sure they have a pleasant face.

Surah Luqman

﴿يُبَنَىَّ أَقِمِ الصَّلَوةَ وَأْمُرْ بِالْمَعْرُوفِ وَانْهَ عَنِ الْمُنْكَرِ
وَاصْبِرْ عَلَى مَآ أَصَابَكَ إِنَّ ذَلِكَ مِنْ عَزْمِ الأُمُورِ –
وَلاَ تُصَعِّرْ خَدَّكَ لِلنَّاسِ وَلاَ تَمْشِ فِى الأُرْضِ مَرَحاً
إِنَّ اللَّهَ لاَ يُحِبُّ كُلَّ مُخْتَالٍ فَخُورٍ﴾

17. O my son! Perform the Salah, enjoin the good, and forbid the evil, and bear with patience whatever befalls you. Verily, these are some of the most important commandments.

18. And turn not your face away from men with pride, nor walk in insolence through the earth. Verily, Allah dislikes the arrogant.

12 Things to Ask a Stranger

1.

What is your purpose here?

Are you sure?

2.

Is your creed closer to ocean or shore?

By sand or by sea have you built your

rapport?

3.

Does your countenance

Counter your core?

Now that I've met

What meets the eye

Is there more?

4.

Do you believe in God?

Yes or no?

If so, which God?

5.

Whether yes or no.

The question is now:

How did you come to know?

That which you know you know?

And are you sure

Of that which you know?

Yes or no?

6.

Whether yes or no.

The question is now:

How imperative is it for me to know?

Rather, for me to believe

That which you know – you know?

And if you know – you know not,

Nor are you sure of that which you know.

Then I ask again: Do you know of God?

Yes or no?

7.

What have your ancestors left you?

What will you leave your predecessors?

8.

What freed you?

What barred you?

What scares you?

What scarred you?

9.

How ugly are you?

Does your ugly

Have an alibi?

What is it?

The ugly?

And the alibi?

10.

Can I trust you?

What corrupts you?

What would cause me to loathe you

After I have loved you?

11.

What are you willing to die for? Live for?

12.

What is your name?

When Opposites Attract

She was the kind of woman folks used to sing about in those old, soulful love songs, the ones that touched your spirit and had its way with it. She was that kind of woman, the kind you noticed with your third eye. The kind of woman that would love a man when he least deserved it. He is the kind of man that least deserved it; the kind of man folks used to sing about in those old, solemn blues songs, the ones that disturbed your spirit and had its way with it. He was that kind of man, the kind that relates courting to basketball, and considers a successful courtship as scoring on the first night. She was the kind of woman that knew his type, the kind of woman that could smell the pompous in a man from a mile away. Yet, she gave him the benefit of doubt. He was the kind of guy that turned a benefit of doubt into casual conversation, and casual conversation into casual sex, the kind of man that could smell the weakness in a woman from a mile away, like blood in lake of piranhas. He was a bad omen, the kind of man that women gave up on the first night. She was the kind of woman that never gave up anyone, the kind of woman that loved selflessly, loved massively, and without reserve. He was the kind of man that worked every nerve, and gave up on women that didn't give him what he wanted the first night, the kind of man that loved with a motive, loved selfishly, with self-interest and self-centeredness. He was that kind of guy, the attention addict, the kind of man that needed his ego stroked by every woman in the room. She wasn't like any other woman in the room. Rather, she was the kind of woman that walked in a place and altered the atmosphere, the kind of woman that made the walls sweat, the hearts sway, the chandeliers gasp, and the women gossip. She was that kind of woman, the kind that folks whispered but never really spoke about, the kind of woman with an aura that mandated the universe's attention. She was that kind of woman, and she did it effortlessly. She did everything effortlessly; she was just that kind of woman. He was the kind of man that always took notice of that kind of woman and went to extremities to woo her. He was just that kind of guy, the kind that cat called to women in passing. He was that kind of guy, the kind you couldn't come to an agreement with on anything. She was the kind of woman that never found palaver in anything, the kind of woman who didn't mind agreeing to disagree. He was the kind of guy that couldn't even agree to that. He was just that kind of guy, the kind that wouldn't ever hold open a door or umbrella for you in the rain. Nevertheless, she was still the kind of woman that never gave up anyone, especially not those whom she loved. And she did, she loved him deeply, with depth and profundity. I suppose that is why she was the kind of woman the men used to sing about in those old, soulful love songs, the kind of woman that could only see the good in people. He was the kind of man that just needed someone to see the good in him, and she did. So he became the kind of man that changed, the kind of man that learned to love back, love selflessly, love massively, and without reserve. After all, he was that kind of man, all along. Love is not about the good things or the bad things we find in people. It is about both. It all depends on where you focus your attention, which makes all the difference.

The Beginning

Love Letter to A Stranger

Dear Stranger,

My soul recognizes your soul. The light in me sees the light in you. The love in me craves the love in you. The truth in me acknowledges the truth in you. The beauty in me admires the beauty in you. My soul honors your soul. I honor the place in you where the entire universe resides. I honor the light, love, truth, beauty, and peace within you, because it is also within me. In sharing these things there is no difference or distance between us. We are united, we are equal, and we are one. I have carried around these splendors within me my entire life, because they are beautiful, they are beautifying, and have embellished my soul. With all the differences we love and celebrate amongst ourselves, it is nice to remember there is something incredibly deep inside you that is the same inside me. For that we are one.

Love,
A Stranger

About The Author

Youssef Kromah aka *Seff Al-Afriqi* is a writer, author, poet, motivational speaker, student, teacher, husband, activist and entrepreneur. He has shared the stage with some the world's most well renowned talents, public figures, activists and legends including Nikki Giovanni, Sonya Sanchez, Common, Talib Kweli, Mos Def, Eve, Wale, Fonzworth Bentley, Kim Coles, Umar Bin Hassan of The Last Poets and countless others.

Youssef is a practicing Muslim and native of West Africa, from the Madingo tribe of Conakry, Guinea. He is the middle child of 13 siblings, and the oldest of five boys. Growing up as a child Afriqi was split between his rich West African, Islamic heritage and the rigid streets of South West Philadelphia. As a result, he found himself in a dichotomy between the streets and what he knew best - Islam.

In his freshman year at Al-Aqsa Islamic Academy, during a stop the violence summit held by the non-profit Peace & Love, Youssef was first introduced to spoken word poetry and it was love at first sight. Since then, he has gone on to feature in HBO's Brave New Voices, author his first book titled "A Gathering of Myself," produce his first EP "The Other Friqi' and a host of many other accomplishments.

Although spoken word poetry has brought Youssef much success, he still holds his education over all other worldly endeavors, as he is an outstanding student of Leadership and Global Understanding at LaSalle University. Seff believes that one day he will be able to truly make an impact on the world through speaking, writing, da'awah and activism, until then he is out spreading truth and working tirelessly to enlighten himself and the entire world around him.

Glossary

Abu Hatim – Muhammad ibn Idris al-Razi was a notable hadith scholar. Al-Dhabbi described him as being an ocean of knowledge.

Abu Hurayrah – also known as `Abdul Rahman ibn Sakhr Al-Azdi was a companion of the Prophet Muhammad and the most quoted narrator of Hadith. Abu Hurayrah spent three years in the company of the Prophet Muhammad and accompanied him on many expeditions and journeys. It is estimated that he narrated around 5,375 ahadith.

Allah – the Arabic word for God, as found in the Quran. Allah is also found in original Biblical scriptures as *Elaha* and in Hebrew Scriptures as *Elohim*.

Da'wah – The word "Da'wah" in Arabic simply means to invite to something. When it is used in an Islamic context it is understood to mean "Inviting to the Way of submission and surrender to one God, Allah."

Divine Decree – or Qadar is the concept of divine destiny in Islam. It is one of the six articles of faith, along with Belief in the Oneness of Allah, the Revealed Books, the Prophets of Islam, the Day of Resurrection and Angels. This concept has also been mentioned in the Quran as Allah's "Decree".

Ibn Hajar – was a medieval Sunni scholar of Islam, who in many regards represents the entire realm of the Sunni world in the field of Hadith.

Ibn Abbas – Abdullah ibn Abbas was a paternal cousin of the Prophet Muhammad. He is honored by Muslims for his unprecedented knowledge of the Quran and profound expertise in Tafsir (exegesis of the Qur'an).

Prophetic Tradition – or Sunnah is the way of life prescribed as normative for Muslims on the basis of the teachings and practices of Prophet Muhammad and interpretations of the Quran. The word Sunnah is derived from the Arabic root *Sanaa* meaning smooth and easy to be followed.

Prophet Muhammad – was a religious, political, social and military leader from Mecca who unified Arabia into a single religious polity under Islam. He is believed to be the final messenger and prophet of God. While many non-Muslims regard Prophet Muhammad to have been the founder of Islam, Muslims understand him to have been the restorer of an unaltered original monotheistic faith of Adam, Noah, Abraham, Moses, Jesus, and all other prophets. Due to his activities as a social reformer, diplomat, merchant, philosopher, orator, legislator, military leader, and philanthropist, Michael H. Hart described him as the most influential human in history.

Qatadah – was one of the companions of the Prophet Muhammad, a member of the Ansar and an esteemed scholar.

Quran – the sacred Islamic book, understood to be the direct word of God, dictated to the Prophet Muhammad by Gabriel and written down in Arabic. The Quran consists of 114 chapters of varying lengths, known as *surahs*.

Rabb- Rabb is an Arabic word meaning Lord, Sustainer, Cherisher or Master, which in an Islamic context refers to Allah.

RAA- Radi'Allahu An – May Allah be immensely pleased with him; this expression follows specifically after uttering the name of any of the companions of Prophet Muhammad.

SAW- Sallah'allahu Alayhi Wasalam – May the peace of Allah be upon him; this expression follows specifically after uttering the name of the Prophet Muhammad.

Taqwa – is the Islamic term that denotes God-consciousness, mindfulness and piety. Its literal meaning is to put a barrier between yourself and the anger of Allah.

UMM-The Arabic word 'Umm' that is used for mother means the root and the foundation of a thing. However, it is so widely used to mean mother that its other meanings are very seldom ever acknowledged.

Mawadah:

The Art of Interlocking Souls – Vol 2

YOUSSEF KROMAH

MAWADAH

The Art of Interlocking Souls Vol. 2

Mawadah:

The Art of Interlocking Souls – Vol 2

Only once in your life, I truly believe, you find someone who can completely turn your world around. You tell them things that you've never shared with another soul, and they absorb everything you say and actually want to hear more. You share hopes for the future, dreams that may never come true, goals that were never achieved and the many disappointments life has thrown at you. When something wonderful happens, you can't wait to tell them about it, knowing that they will share in your excitement. They are not embarrassed to cry with you when you are hurting or laugh with you when you make a fool of yourself. Never do they hurt your feelings or make you feel like you are not good enough, but rather they build you up and show you the things about yourself that make you special and even beautiful. There is never any pressure, jealousy or competition but only a quiet calmness when they are around. You can be yourself and not worry about what they will think of you because they love you for who you are. The things that seem insignificant to most people such as a note, poem or long walk become invaluable treasures kept safe in your heart to cherish forever. Memories of your childhood come back and are so clear and vivid it's like being young again. Colors seem brighter and more brilliant. Laughter seems part of daily life where before it was infrequent or didn't exist at all. A phone call or two during the day helps to get you through a long day's work and always brings a smile to your face. In their presence, there's no need for continuous conversation, but you find you're quite content in just having them nearby. Things that never interested you before become fascinating because you know they are important to this person who is so special to you. You think of this person on every occasion and in everything you do. Simple things bring them to mind like a pale blue sky, gentle wind or even a storm cloud on the horizon. You open your heart knowing that there's a chance it may be broken one day and in opening your heart, you experience a love and joy that you never dreamed possible. You find that being vulnerable is the only way to allow your heart to feel true pleasure that's so real it scares you. You find strength in knowing you have a true friend and possibly a soul mate who will remain loyal to the end. Life seems completely different, exciting and worthwhile. Your only hope and security is in knowing that they are a part of your life.

To Be Continued...

Don't miss out on the next book by your favorite author. Visit www.seffalafriqi.com and sign our mailing list for the latest news, updates, and merchandise! Thanks for your undying support and loyalty.

Facebook: Seff Al-Afriqi
YouTube: Seff Al-Afriqi
Instagram: @SeffAlAfriqi
Twitter: @SeffAlAfriqi

Made in the USA
San Bernardino, CA
23 December 2013